Mortals, Myths, and Maybes

Poetry by McKenna Graf
writing over the word limit

Film by McKenna Graf
Lost Conversations

Mortals, Myths, and Maybes

McKenna Graf

Editor: Dakota Reed
Cover Design: McKenna Graf
Layout: McKenna Graf
Design Consult: Gayle Hendricks

Published by: Parisian Phoenix Publishing

Printed in the U.S.A
First Edition: 2024
ISBN: 978-1-957863-26-9

For adolescence.
Here you whisper to me once more.

TABLE OF CONTENTS

PART ONE: YOUTH

i'm just a writer, i write things down

i don't like speaking up
        because the words never
                seem to catch up
        with how fast
           the
    wheels   in my
     brain   are
        turning,
i feel a (burning
        inside me
                to have people hear my thoughts).
but i need time
        to select
                my words
        carefully
                so that when my words are on the page
                    they can reach through
                        and grab hold of people's emotions
        and kiss and hug them
    until they see things
a different way.

        i want my words to be stained
on the white pages of a book
                and in turn stained on the reader's heart.
        i want my words to be part of their lives
for more than the moment when I'm speaking.

If i can write my words down
        the ink will
                swim
        in their

                    mind's
                                    eye
begging them to go back
and absorb every
                        drop,
                                every
                                    detail on the page.
Because as their fingers touch
the pages, so should the pages
have touched them. all

            i want
is to be a great writer,
                    a great thinker. So that i
                can arrange words and my
sentences will be great.

Help me be great,
i whisper to my pen and paper,
Help me believe,

                    You and me can be great,
                    they sing to my fingers
                    through the symphony of words
                    flowing out of me

Remeeting Autumn

The warmth of the sun is slowly siphoned
into her skin throughout the summer,
so that when autumn comes
her warm body is protected from
the cold breeze that settles over the earth.

But the tans fade from her skin
and the sands of the beaches slip
through her fingers,
replaced by the loud crunch as she
steps on orange and red leaves
that fall onto the freshly trimmed grass.

Her tongue craves the
seasonal scents and
her skin whispers asking for more
layers and layers and you lay her
down gently as her
body prepares—
remembering, remembering—
and slips into autumn again.

18 and Looking Back

I remember screams meshing with laughs,
bare feet slapping on the floor as I run
with a naked doll clutched in my hand.

I remember pretending,
wishing,
hoping,
I was OLDER.
I was always the mom when we played "house."

I remember laughing at every single thing you said.

I remember crying when I had no friends.

I remember Christmases with my family,
when I felt more love than I could fit in my (hands,
it
overflowed

and
tickled my toes).

I remember reading about fairies from Pixie Hollow,
and my first book— a dragon's egg rolling away from home.

I remember never wanting to leave home,
clinging to my mom's leg.

(If I just hold tight enough!)

I remember my first day of kindergarten,
the smells of glue and goldfish still stuck in my nose.

I remember the way my hands excitedly scribbled
across a page,
when I asked someone to be my best friend.

I remember the *stupid* happiness I felt when she said
yes.

I remember dancing aimlessly with my sisters,
the moonlight pouring through the living room windows.

I remember pretending to hold textbooks in my
arms,
as I walked the halls of my pretend high school.

how quickly I will walk out of my real high school,
into a new journey where high school will be what

I'm remembering,

(If I just hold tight enough!)

I don't remember saying goodbye to my childhood,
but on this page I give it a kiss and a hug.

you always were mine,
you'll always be mine.

goodnight,
I'll see you under the next moon.

Castle of Cardboard Part I

There's a place that used to be safe:
a castle made out of cardboard
      with rules written in chalk,
            easily washed away or remade.
The scariest thing was the rain.

Count 10 seconds to the next strike,
      it's God bowling above.

Count the sheep,
      don't be a freak, drink this
          and you'll fall
              asleep.

    The clock chimes
  and the tide washes in,
alone on an island
from a stubborn independence
that I now regret making.

Burn out then   blackout,

I could never juggle well in gym
and I hated learning to swim
all because I could never win.

She thinks I enjoy the prize
more than the game,
but instant gratification leads
to undeserved satisfaction.

I want to build an empire out of

moments and games with clear rules,
but I'm stuck
in a Jenga set
and every move I make
threatens destruction.
I don't know how to live
for myself, stuck in this (limbo
of what's mine and what is
decidedly not.
)
My independence

is a ruse. I'm still on my knees
for you and I'm honoring,
worshiping, and wondering
why that still doesn't feel
enough.

Falling down a rabbit hole of—
what if— as I'm only curious
about my downfall and how
far must I fall before
I realize all I've lost
out of fear of being
too much? Am I
not giving eno-
ugh? Is this
even eno-
ugh?

Oldest Child Syndrome

I'm drawing a highway out of chalk
until it dwindles down
               to my fingertips
and my nails are dragging
across the concrete. I'm making
the path for you
to enjoy and succeed, but I'm
laying myself down in the unknown,
carving out the way,
          carving out myself,
               (be careful not to trip on
                       my bones)
letting myself get cut,
just so you don't.

I cruised down the highway but
tunneled to an end, rushed ahead and
avoided any exits. Took our routes of
fantasy too seriously. I'm here you see—

I perpetually put you first,
so that now as I'm faced with something
I so *desperately* want
I don't know how to ask for it.

My voice
        dwindles
            down
                   like
                       the
                           chalk,
vocal chords unused and

yet, still bloodied.

My eyes well with tears
for the words unsaid.
The paths I've paved for you
blossom with flowers and ferns,
but the ones I never paved for myself
are overgrown with weeds and thorns,
making me bleed for the times I didn't turn

and I'm not sure I'll ever learn—
Because even if you told me the heads
were cut off the flowers
and the ferns overgrown,
I still laid out the path like a red carpet for you.

And maybe you never even asked for it,
but you counted on me like the sun
and slept peacefully while I struggled to rise.

Guilt of Growing Up

Prostrate me to the ground
and I'd beg for forgiveness
for all the places I've ripped myself from
and the experiences I've missed out on.
Roll your eyes at me and guilt me for moving on
when I thought I was being strong.

I'll dramatize every eye roll and car ride missed,
I'm in a black box trying to find the light of my future,
but the warmth of my past keeps me from moving on.
I'm addicted to comfort and there's no patches
to restrain me from using it until the last drop.

But I'm lighting candles and letting the dead rest
where they lay. I've built a church and started laying
offerings to myself, when will it be enough?

I'm picking the cards of my future and I want you.
Death isn't the end, it's a whisper of something new.
Take my hand like we do when we cross the street,
Let's see if we can find ourselves something sweet.

Mirrored Hearts

I look in the mirror and see myself,
see the lines of legacy, I see you and
all the places you've been before—
my eyes, my hair, my nose
passed down from you to me.

Invisibly your spirit burns inside me,
enlightening so many pieces of you in me,
every truth I deny myself and
lie I wish I could tell is reflected
right back in your eyes.

I can't ever pretend in front of you.
You've been everywhere I'll ever be
so you're the hand that knows
how to calm me down from my flames,
and keep me from the wood, words, whatever I can't outrun.

We're a match of taking things too literally
and getting anxious over the choices we make.
And just as easily as the wind blows can our match be lit,
but there's no one else I'd rather burst into flames with.
That's how I know, if a father was something you choose,
my heart would call out to you.

i (wish i could)

i keep drops of golden sunlight in my hair,
      let them drip from the top of my head
            down to my toes.
i cleanse my skin with the river water,
      a body anew.
i run my hands through the dirt and grass,
      twirl flowers between my fingers.
i taste the season in the air,
      on my lips, on my neck: the wind.
i dip my foot in the clouds,
      watch it dissipate beneath me
         sweet mist, *complete me.*
i wish to dance across the world
      with dainty fingers,
and sink into the earth
      (I'll leave my old life behind
         for my soul has been dipped in gold)

Your Laugh Licks Out Like Flames

Your laugh licks out like flames and your hands
extend into claws that never release.
You shove a string down my throat when you talk to me
and when I'm running in circles to break free
                        you laugh
                and sing
        ring
around   *the*
        rosy,
                        pocketful
        of reasons
and treasons you
pretend to care
 about.

So deep inside your own utopia
you force your hand in mine
and try to drown me along,
and when I scream of the pain
you shove me further down,
mistaking the wreckage
for an offering of problems
for you to fix and force
into love.

I am not a stage for you to perform and
practice and use so I will live in the world
and you can remain in the wings
giggling about the ways, the whys, the whens,
whatever you decide will bring you the most wins.

My Immortality

I am the fairytale that never ends,
the selkie that never runs out of skins to shed
and the phoenix that never needs more flames.

I know how to live as gracefully as the fae of the Seelie court
and live as dangerously as those of the Unseelie.

I am a thousand oddities and lost things and
legends tied together by a desire to capture
what's behind the second star to the right.

I'm young and invincible.

I will live forever in the stories
that have touched my soul and
the ones that my heart has created.

Loving Layli

Love as gentle as a river,
I long to touch your banks
and feed your lakes.
Only with you can I be in content memory
for Lovesick has been no friend to me.

PART TWO: DESTRUCTION

3 Broken Loves of the Gods

1.   Achilles and Patroclus

The river swallows your chaos whole and at the bottom you can finally breathe. Like an immortal god you go under the water with open eyes and clean skin. An image one could only wish to create.

I want whispers from you in the night and kisses in the morning, he whispers.
But the sun is dying, I whisper back.

2.   Orpheus and Eurydice

Never let me meet the kiss of death. The beautiful monstrous deity she is. She stands before the gates of the Underworld and allows people to live forever in the elusive Elysium.

Take my hand and I'll tell you all about it, he whispers.
So long as you promise never to look away, she whispers back.

The voices in his head are screaming too loud to think, eyes burning from being denied sight. There's something cold caressing his skin. Comforting self doubt. Demanding to be touched.

I'm going to reach out towards you, he whispers.

She meets death.

3. Hades and Persephone

It was cold, exacting and now it is dying itself.

To feel the warmth of the sun in my hand would be nice, he
whispers, *like an embrace after isolation.*
Let me take my love and put it over you like a blanket, she
whispers back.

It's summer. I saw someone who was lonely.

Ode To Sirens

Your golden hair and sparkling skin is wasted
on men who want nothing more than sin,

Listen, to me, my dear,
You are here between my words,

Let me be your voice,
The one beating in your soul,

Not the one laced with words to bring the men in from shore,
Your power runs strong in your golden veins and angelic
voice,

Wicked as the witches that burned along your sands,
Rise up in my lungs to avenge the ones who didn't have a
choice,

You are as strong as the waves you call home,
And you are so much more than the "vindictive whore,"

More powerful than the men that fall to your knees,
Your scales tell more tales than they can comprehend,

Let me be the one to rewrite your fairytale,
Let us sail towards the narrative of strong women,

For we wear your title of "daughters of the devil" with pride,
A man doesn't hold our power inside.

Mad Musings on Majnun

Tragic love doomed from the start,
Weighs down on an already heavy heart.

        Testing the limits of loyalty;
        Surely you'll be evermore to me, like royalty.

    Our love is humble and strong
    Don't we remain steady when things go awry?

        And yet you won't survive either way
        She sucks you dry to give you a reason to
        stay.

            Who will make it all worth
            it?
            Who stands on the pulpit?

        Because it stands in adoration
        And there appears to be no hope of
        reconciliation.

    Love is not a thing you can search for
    But a feeling that possesses you to your core.

Lost in this suffering and pain
She'd call it love's loyalty and keep him on the chain.

I Confused Promises for Vows

I used to worship at the altar of promises.
I'd slit my throat on the throne of loyalty
and let the blood solidify what I thought words could not.

But you convince me my voice holds the power
of the sirens, through intention phrases become
rules and by them I will always abide.

Even when my tongue gets cut out
to my demise, I will see through
what I've sworn for you.

And I will raise my sword to defend what is mine.
I'm still learning how to grip the sword from its rock,
but it doesn't mean I'm not trying.

If not through action, I have laid my life
down in the ink I whispered to you.
There was no one else I'd rather open my heart to.

And I don't want to love hard again if it's not you
that I fall into.
I couldn't really, seeing as how I fell on the

sword I was trying to raise for you.
I asked for what was mine but
what was mine didn't ask for me.

A lot, a lot, a lot
and I lost.
We joked about people we know fading into the past

because they were better there anyways.
Funny how that story doesn't feel the same here,
now that we too, didn't last,

but still I hold onto you like a last breath.
Because I still wonder–
It's the curse of a wanderer

through space and time.
I fixate on a number, a cycle,
a rhyme. Torn–

Is it my turn to sit in the storm?

I'll wait and wait
until the world is in flames
and I don't even know my own name

but yours will still be brandished on my tongue.
And yet I only whisper your name,
I sing to you with my supposed silent siren song.

But I'll never be able to confess it loudly again,
that was reserved for when I beamed with love.
And yet I still whisper, whisper, whisper it to myself.

I wonder again,
Will you come back one day like you do in my dreams?
But my heart doesn't beat enough

for me to believe that will come true.
Despite the sacrifices I made to our love,
you slayed our string instead of risking resentment

but really all it feels like you did was poison the ground
where our roots were growing.
But maybe time will wash over us

like an ocean and heal our roots.
Maybe I'll forget the day I lost faith in promises,
because everyday I find shockingly colored flowers

growing amidst the poison;
signs I can't make sense of
but that tickles at my mind.

But you said, "I'll see you soon,"
and that's the stupid hope that drags me back

down.

I've Sold My Soul to the Devil

I've sold my soul to the Devil
and now my pen belongs to his false god,
Love. How the world brings such offerings
to her— they tear out half
their hearts and claim it's finally full
when they drink her in.

I could drown in a sea of the so-called-lovely cliches
the dearest devil has given me to use,
I've choked on every always
and vomited at the amount of forevers I've seen.
She's had an altar erected in her favor,
and the Devil adorns it with roses.

He seems to think I can write him intertwined
with her and you see I tried.
I forced my heart into his
just the same as the others,
I dutifully put on the rose colored glasses
given to me at the gates, I recited
cliches as if I knew no other words–

> It's with you I wanna take on the world.
> Let's jump in the car and follow the moon.

The devil was never here,
the devil was never you.

I swore myself to you with my eyes wide open
but you had sacrificed yourself to this false god
long before I'd ever known you.

I wish I could say there was some grievous sin on your part,
I'd love to let you fully embody the persona of the so-called
King of Sins. But the worst thing you did was fall
in love with love and realize that wasn't me
before I could. Now I grapple with the deals you made
and look for the pieces of me I chiseled

                                down

        and   rearranged
                for   you.
I find them in you where we made our deal
and I flee, making as little footprints as I can
cringing at the idea of you following me.

I thought I sold my soul to the devil
but really it just crumpled at your feet.
I spend all my time villainizing you,
all you did was romanticize me,
but I'm tired of cursing you and false gods.

I want to find the real love hidden
(between heaven and hell),
I want to be able to be spoken to
in rhythms and rhymes
that soothe my heart
and believe that it's true.

i wish i didn't think at all

they tell me to stop
thinking about you, to
stop giving him that power
(i wish i didn't think at all)

but when did writing become powerless?
i refuse to reassociate,
there's more power in reclamation.
(i wish i didn't think at all)

you infested my mind
with your sugary cliches,
(i wish i didn't think at all)

i refuse to let those inconsistencies
live on in the way i immortalized you.
(i wish i didn't think at all)

if you are to remain on the page
it will represent the way you left
and i'm allowed to write it in flames,
(i wish i didn't think at all)

especially when you cared less about my name
and more about making me care.
(i wish i didn't think at all)

call me bitter or accuse me of
playing the victim but i'm entitled
to hate you just as you were to break me.
(i wish i didn't think at all)

now from the cracked porcelain i rise
stronger than the delicate doll you praised.
(i wish i didn't think at all)

so i'll begrudgingly murmur my thanks
but I'll never let you forget
what a mistake it was to leave
the way you did.
(i wish i didn't think at all)

i hope the next girl you latch onto
looks more like your mother
maybe then you'll realize
what you confused our love for

and you'll wish you couldn't think at all.

In Loving Memory

I've been picking at my skin,
mostly the hangnails on my fingers
and all the acne I can find on my face.
I figure the more I pull, the
less
skin
there
will
be left that's been touched by you.

My lips have become so chapped
and so many layers have dried off
that they're not even the same ones
that touched yours.

And now my hair has been
drenched in blood,
and washed out pink.
That wasn't meant to be a declaration of war,
I just couldn't look at the hair you used to love anymore.

And there's a cut
on my hand.
The same one you used to
hold.
Inside the cut are
rocks you left behind
that I'm struggling to pick
out;
struggling even more to decide between
throwing them
back

                    at
                                    you
                        or
            swallowing
        them
whole.

You left me lying in a place that has no ground
and I don't care how loudly my actions echo
because out here they'll never reach you.
So I'm peeling the cut
            on my hand (open
and dragging
            off
                the
                    rest
                        of
                        my
                                skin
            and it's unbearable
weight.

I am muscle and blood.
But soon my heart stops
pumping and the blood no longer
                                        runs.
Then my muscles

                    shrink

                                from disuse
and my organs
                                        leave
            in grief.

Until I
am just
bones.

Brittle and bare, I step outside
        and even if it were sunny I'd feel only

             the wind.

My feet are unsteady
     walking
     on a tight-
     rope of
     the string
     that used
     to connect
     us. But I've
     fallen
         off
           of
              it,

or maybe you pushed me off.

But I feel the string
       wrap
 around   my
       ankle,
and then rises the miserable hope
that it means you still care. But I just stare
as it tightens around me,
until it's cut too deep

and now I have no

                        feet

to slow myself down

            and so I

                 start to

                         fall.

Embracing the cold hands
pulling me further
        down
            into
                the
                    dark.

Despite the numbness in my heart,
I'll write sonnets in my blood
under those glowing ghost spots
      swirling
          around.
   Ghost spots
               of memories,
     of dancing in love.

I thought I mastered the art, but now
dancers turned to ghosts,
they're intangibility taunting me,
my naive happiness mocking me.

I write about how we made promises in the car,
like when you said you loved me
and I wrote in the word *forever*.

Now I hear ghostly moans of you telling me
till death do us part.
I guess this is what it feels like to be buried alive.

I grab an oar

and I ignore you
because I adored you.
Getting closer was the hardest

going through loops I didn't see
finding spaces that were left
for me.

You said you ignored me
because you adored me
but how does that reflect

how you want us to be?
Ignore me because you adore me
and teach me I must

shock a crowd to turn
a head.
Train me to crave that instead.

And shed every warning
and shroud myself in
armor and battle

for war and more.
Are you sure?
Sure you don't just want

something to hold?
An oar you can grab
and chase some good-boy points?

Make me read every mind

and promise all the time.
Pin me down to

show me you'll let me back up.
Show me you're tough,
because to you, you're not

enough, of the declarations of love,
love, and love
whoever's standing in front of you.

You lost your vision,
hands right in front of you,
I turned my head

                    and you grabbed me instead.

Learn all my body language
and damage my memories
to break

a wall in to your fantasies
and my bed.
I wonder if you felt

skin or a girl.
I'll curl
            in
                to
        you
because
there's chains rattling in my head,

but they were never locked.

Fetish

Bringing out the worst in each other
you said it's good to fall in love with a writer
because then you'll never die.

As if you knew you'd need immortalizing.
Waiting until my heart is complete and set with
love for you to eat and give yourself,

the cannibal to my necrophiliac.
You die in bliss eating the love you've taken from others
but expect me to maintain the love for you,
you took out of my heart.

What am I meant to do with your lifeless corpse?
Weep until my tears give you a life that you didn't want?
How am I supposed to love someone
with one foot out the door?

My love was pity to keep you inside,
but I'm the one still stuck here, while you've played
with my heart like a selfish toddler at a playground.

You've taken control of my words with selfish desires
but I maintain my intentions
and will let them expose you to fire.

A Sinner's Sonnet

My frail body kneels at an altar that will soon deny me.
I crawl back bloodied and break bread in my bed.
Enter the hurried whispered confession: *Please*
don't let this sin infect. The choir sings: *He sees you*

dead. They tell me we all have our own crosses to bear.
Mine both a cross and what's boarded up doors to homes.
I thought my parents kept me from you out of fear.
Now I see it was to keep me from putting myself on the stone.

Self-sacrificing was in my nature. Never question why.
Sheets of sins were passed out. Everyone looked at the sinner.
I chained myself to the burning pew and I
let the worst sins of mine be stripped bare for dinner.

You're eating the parts of me you molded
and made. Find it bitter and cringe
at the consequence. You won't feel scolded
and are still screaming of scalding heat. Hinge

me as your sacrifice to the faith you cling to as you
put me on the altar. How quickly fear becomes worship too.

i've known death by

a thousand papercuts
forming on my hands.
each time i pick up this page
a trickle of blood,

                         drips
with every
           you
that i use.

i reopen a wound
that was hard enough
to sew closed to begin with.
but there's ten thousand unanswered questions

and books filled with plans.
i can't tell if its me that's paper thin
or that the words
                     you
left me with

were really knives in disguise.
i've picked apart the love from the hate
and let myself fester in the anger
            you've
created.

i'm not entirely sure what's true anymore
except that
                  you're
gone

and i no longer care
and i wish
                    you'd
stay there. i wish the pain didn't fester,

i wish the words didn't remember,
i don't understand why
i can't write about anything else.
why did

                    you
make
an expectation that
                                        you

needed to be the sun?
was
          your

ego so big that

                    you
needed me to
suffer that bad if
                    you

ever took
          your
light?
                              you

forgot that i thrive
 in darkness alone, i've never needed
anyone else but my own.

EXCUSE MY DRAMATICS

I can pick a singular characteristic
          and   plan
        a   whole
      future   around
         it
letting the red flags be the backdrop
to the love I imagine for us
and only the biggest fracture could shatter
the reality I've created. Even still
I'd try to duct tape it back together
because at least then I'd have control.
Whereas now I feel that
        I'm lost unmoored
          as if I don't feel my feet on the floor
    walking me in the direction that my eyes face.

It's true I barely feel my heart beat nowadays
but by no means have I lost myself.
I will sharpen her into a weapon
that will make even the hardest bleed.
Time may soften my edges
but I've learned my lesson in erecting
barriers around my heart
and misplacing my trust.

Excuse my dramatics,
excuse my all or nothing attitude,
excuse the fact that I felt forever fall
 on top of me like an avalanche (
        I'm suffocating
      underneath
      but clawing my way out.

But call me dramatic I dare you.
)
I hope this new version of me scares you.

Ballad for My Partner

If I were a British male poet,
you could curse me to never read again,

or hear the soft lilts of another song,
and I know you won't ask,

but I'd rather give up my skin
and burn my muscles in the sun,

lose every organ I could ever give
and lie down in the ground

than stop loving you and our life.
And though it may not have started yet—

God knows it hasn't—
I'd give everything for the life we haven't yet lived.

Because now that I've gotten a taste of
domestic life with you,

I've let adoration become mourning
and I'm stuck in the ground

clawing around
missing all that my hands passed through,

digging to try and find you again.
I've taken my flaming skin off,

lost my eyes to dirt
and cut my ears on rocks.

I'm in the earth to be closer to you
and your roots,

I'm stuck in a poem and
lost in love.

You've gone and all the words I
forgot to say

seep into the page.
But I'll read this to you today,

I'll write to you tomorrow,
there's not a dramatic musing

I haven't thought about you,
but there's not a thought

I haven't told to you.
No matter how far you get

and how far I fall to the ground,
there always lies a string

and on the other end you can be found.

Sip It Dry

I reach for the moon
the way the sunflower
                        does the sun.
I feel my soul
            slipping
                    away
with every incline of my head
to look up at the sky.
I wonder why I see the stars
 as the dead dancing
                        in
        my
                    mind.

I don't know where we go when we die
but I imagine jumping   on   clouds
                        like   pillows
and painting the sky with blue,
letting it
            drip
                into
                    rain.

I see Apollo dragging the day away into night.
I see my hands
                    nervously touching the deep navy
and watching it ripple
                        into
            dancing
                    ribbons.
I feel the scars the living world left
on my back. I stack my trauma

into a backpack, dropping it
                    on-
            to   the
        high-   est
            mountain.

                              I'm weightless
                              here,
                    despite fearing the unknown,
        away from the only home i've ever known.

I've sewn and stitched myself into a thousand different faces.

I'm pacing in front of a lake in the sky,
            it holds my mind,
                    peels back
                layers of my skin
            displays the mind I've always lived with;
I scoop it up and drink it dry.

Stuck in a, well,

I'm used to being accused of a thousand mistakes
when I've barely made one. I'm used
to being tested for loving good enough
when "I love you" should be sufficient.
I'm used to baring my skin and having it cut into pieces
and being shown the massacre as evidence of his love.

And I'm being haunted by all the fights we don't have,
I'm waiting for a bomb to drop and
 find that you wrote my name on it.
I'm waiting for everything I am to have not been enough,
you're waiting for me to suddenly not see you anymore
and I'm waiting for you to decide you've seen enough and
crucify me for everything I've done or didn't do
according to a set of rules you hide in the corner.

Because I was the virgin Mary he put on a pedestal
for being so strong and pure, honored
for a false sense of the cleaness of my lips
and the delicacy of my skin. I was all he could eat
and devour and absorb and I'm

borrowing trouble from past pains
and now I'm trying to dig myself out of the well.
But once the tears break
            through, and comparison
                        rains down
                in a storm and rivers
                            of doubt roll in, I'm
being swallowed whole and I'm

                        drowning,

but instead of cutting myself on rocks
in the hopes of making it drain, I'm trying to
learn how to swim and so I

take my hand away from the ledge
and push my glasses up my nose.
I'll drown in *what if*
if I don't learn to breathe underwater.

I walk away from the well
and dive into the lake.

People Pleaser Paradox

Over and over again I come to this altar,
I stab knives into my ears so I can open them up
and listen better– see, I've heard enough tales of martyrs,
had their names drilled in my mind
to believe that the greatest thing I could do is be one.
And yet I'd slip into it easily, play my role dutifully,

Repeat after me and remember,
I'm a martyr who should die for others,
prostrate myself at their feet again and again
for a crime I don't remember committing.

But somewhere along the way the definition of martyr got
lost,
                         and I picked up *victim* instead.
Instead I crucify myself because no one else will.
I nail my spirit
               down
until I'm tamed and perfect for the world.

And my ears bleed
             until
      I can't
                   hear
          at all
and I'm
                            lost
     in the
         rush
            of blood
and I cut out my eyes
to avoid sinning again.

The Conditions

I've been conditioned to think that
every time someone's walls break
I need to pick up all the pieces off the floor.
Pieces I get blamed for cracking without touching
and I fear that I'll just break them even more.

I've been conditioned to think that
every time someone's walls break
I needed to have loved better,
better would have been calling and
letting love tumble out of my mouth when I don't
know where it's running, even if it was performance
at least it'd keep your heart running.

I've been conditioned to think that
like a dog you'll leave the dead bird at my feet,
lick me so that the blood stains my hands and not yours
but still you'll be clawing for more.

And I hate this repetition of conditions,
hysterics, and spirals that wrap
                              around
                                        my
              throat
and constrict my voice from whispering how scared
I am that one day you'll regret all the effort
you put into someone bruised and battered.

And even though I'd do the same for you,
I should have been better than all
those who caused pain to you. I don't allow
myself the smallest mistake, but I wish

I could give myself the same grace
as the one you ceaselessly give.

And I'd die in this cycle of running and risking
everything I have to placate someone else.
But you've pulled me from the riptide
and I've swam to shore risking my pride and more,
but I know you'll hold me like I'm your world.

Throwing and Catching Stars

I've been left alone with words,
the ability to bend them becoming a curse,
the weight feels
                        crushing
and the dread compares to nothing.
I'm grasping at   straws
but the pain still   gnaws.
I   strain
  to see if you're still there
and I see silhouettes of my heart
                        bare
and   there
                                    and here
                and where
                                                I am.
I'm beating against time like a battering ram
trying to reverse and hold you again,
but you whisper promises of walks along the Seine.

And now I've confused myself,
in my chaos I've bruised myself,
because I don't need promises unknown
or hands held till they're sewn.
What I want is you and your complications and complexities.
What I want is us and our differences and propensities.

Our inherent and unconditional and stupid love is all I need.
I ask nothing more of you than this love that is true and can
lead
me to a time where we don't have to worry
        about planes
                        and trains

and all the walks
that surely we'd take to get to each other.
Soon that won't be a bother,
just love me like the stars,
and we'll shine just like they're ours.

PART THREE: REBIRTH

Rebirth

I'm trying to wear my insecurities as confident
as flames move unto themselves
but somehow still I give you the power
to douse them in waves. I've laced my hair
with the pearls of the sky but my manufactured curls
          are
                        wrapping
      around
              my
     throat,
leaving bruises behind.
Everything I adorn myself with
is the object of your scorn.
The stars that I swallow are filled
with my lust for life and I let your eyes
with knives turn them into throwing stars
scarring my throat as they go down. The flowers
that grew from my skin now look like an overgrown
 garden of vines and thorns and flowers that
                                   have no place
       here.

Here, you see my shadow,
                    underneath the ink,
lion lurking in the night.
Every word I don't have the courage to say out loud
but inside I've found (the
                    yellow brick road
          and I roar
)
on the page. Here,
you see me reading this poem

                              the naive prey
                exposed
                                      in the day.
        Do you see the way my cheeks go red?
        And I can't look anyone in the eyes?
        I can't even open my mouth because

my lips don't hold the same confidence my heart does,
they can't find the
                              rhythm
that it beats so surely.

Because I live in the (inbetween),
                    the upside down
                         the never
                                         found.

I dance in the sky,
        my head in the clouds,
                and when I look around
                        I lose my grip of the moon and

crash to the earth.
I slip into a vat
        of ink that
                covers me,
                body and soul.
                              I'm drowning but
                my hands crawl out and
        my fingerprints stain the ground.

In the sky I could stand here
                         bare
                                with nothing

but a dress of tears and sweat
but here you are perpetually aware
of my existence,
of my differences
compared to your mythical norm.

Down here I must cover myself with ink.
Ignore the burn,
the way the ink simmers below my skin.
I'll use my calloused feet to spark a blaze anyways.

You can't exist in both,
It whispers thickly,
Down here it's ink or the world, there is no inbetween.
Choose or its ash you'll become.

I have
no place
down here, my
musings sound like nonsense
and my outfits are for Halloween.
I can only exist how I want in words and whispers
and want.   *Didn't you know? Having things out*
of
reach builds character, makes you
strong.

But even if I was as strong as the
witches and
sirens
that sing in my veins
we'd reach the same fate.
The only thing we're guaranteed to
reach

                              is death itself,
And I reach
                a sword that wields my disintegration
just because I couldn't choose a world.

Little do they know
liberation is the greatest thing you could give a witch.
Now I can go back to my spells in the sky
without your earthly perceptions weighing me
                                              down.

So stab me now and watch my insecurities pour
                                        out with
                        the blood
        and skin searing into ash.
    I'll be unrecognizable,
from ashes I will become the flames.

This Love is Mine

It's not the holding you so close you can barely
breathe or letting a stubborn potter mold us
together or touching you places the world
has never seen just for the thrill of it.

It's the look that friends don't give each other,
it's the silent echo of "more" that hums inside.
Even when your eyes are glued to me
still bartering for more moments,
more time writing you and me until it becomes
us in a way that defies places.

It's different because coming to you
should feel like home no matter where we are.
It's different because my heart was a stone
and now it's alive overthinking and
                        sinking
                                in definitions that don't
                                    make sense and thinking,
                                        no one's ever felt this before.

But no I've gone down that road and I was scorned,
no, in truth it echoes of couples past
and I've seen them make it last.
And I know if it were to come to pass,
after our last, under whatever circumstances that may be
I'd hear the echo of millions of hearts crash
                                    before my own.
                    But still it echoes,
it murmurs for more.

The beauty of love isn't feeling like

no one has ever felt this before.
It's sticking your tongue out for communion
and savoring what millions have felt before;
Falling
            into the first thing humans learned to do
      and never tried to make more than this
wanting.

Echoes of love is what we swim under
making new tides
and how long that will last isn't up to us.
But I'll enjoy the sun on my face or my back.
I'll let your hands become the waves
            and the sand, my body.
                  I'll meet you relentlessly at the shore,
            there's nothing more I need to be sure of.
      So, love I release you from the clutches of my grasp,
            I'll let you wash over me whenever that comes to
pass.

Good morning and

say hi to my body,
I haven't seen her in a while.
I've been running in circles
and building up towers,
I neglected her on the ground
in the dirt, in the mulch.

Say hi to my soul,
I've been writing about them more.
the multitudes and mysteries they hold.
My brain has deformed and the thoughts have less hold
and hold me please while I daydream.
I'm afraid I'll lose all hold on the world,
so I nail my feet to the ground and feel,

some lingering fear of what happens when I let myself free.
When I stop thinking what's next,
when I can stay present without being stuck to the ground,
when my soul, *say hi*, can hover in the in between
holding on to my body, *say hi*, and ride on bubbles and
dreams.

Castle of Cardboard Part II

My eyes dart in so many directions
all the time, but now I find myself
locked on your eyes
not understanding why.

*How many questions do I have to ask
to convince myself you'll stay?*

Embrace change and unknowns
and remain because it feels right,
not because I think know how it'll end
not because of the rights and
wrongs circling
                around
                      in
             my
  head.

*When will I be able to trust
my heart again?*

I refuse to over-romanticize and dramatize again
so I find myself afraid to feel.
But I am a poet that lives in extremes—
tears and fears are inevitable,
but so are lazy smiles and talking for hours.

Isn't forever hard to come by?

but forever seems more and more a feeling
than a measurement
and I want to find it with you,

whatever that means,
whatever it seems,

I'm breaking myself out of
       the interrogation room
             of my mind
and building a new castle
with every emotion I could hope to feel,
giving the crown to the drama queen
and not being afraid to be seen as just that.

I Used to Live in a Glass Castle

I was conditioned to believe that
all conflict is my fault, fueling
the desire to end my own happiness
as I'm always anxiously anticipating the end,
How could I be content?

And I'm sick of the expectations
and conflations of what we should do.
I'm sick of hearing *should, would, could,*
never *I want* or *let's do,*
Do you feel content?
In this glass castle you'll come to resent?
I resent your your your,

but even if I avoid the strike
there's still a bloody end
and I'm blamed for not taking it seriously enough.
And now I don't trust
the gentle guiding hand on my back,
constantly waiting for the scars to bleed again.

But how am I supposed to show
that we have the thickest skin
if it never cracks?

You set fire to every bomb
I warned you not to touch
and claimed you were just trying to get
them out of the way.

You'd watch as I stitched myself back up again
and you'd call us strong from the sidelines.

Our so-called love was a
manufactured volcano at a science fair:
fake, volatile and short-lived.

I need a love like the ocean,
as strong as she is gentle
and relentlessly reaching for the sand
no matter how hard it may seem to stay.

Aimlessly wander along the beach and
laugh and love and pick up seashells with me,
I no longer want to scream in flames.

The Riddles

Lately I've been speaking to myself in riddles,
wondering how my heart has
                  unraveled
                      into
              a
                  ribbon,
            now
                  tangled
          in
              my
          hair
and my brain has become
                puzzle
                  pieces,
      out
         of
    place
and
broken as it
      drowned in waters
  I didn't understand.
But now the oceans
            and rivers
                and lakes
                    are fading into
                puddles
and I'm learning to dance and   jump!
          and   swim!   and

I'm finding that what made it hard to breathe underwater
wasn't because it hurt, but because I was alone.
But now I'm above and below and in between

and I'm letting my soul slip from my skin,

but I'm afraid of what happens when/
                                    if/
                                            I let it
                                    go too far.
What happens when I get too close to the sun?
What happens when I've flipped my skin inside out
and just made it easier for it to be ripped apart?

But I've burned and I've bled and I've screamed
so loud my voice has broken down to a whisper.
I was afraid of what would happen when I was actually heard,
afraid that my wants and needs would be more than I deserve.
Stuck in a cycle of getting less because I can't ask for more,
I'm sure of nothing and everything and
I'm afraid of everything I do
            and you could absolutely break my heart.

I'm afraid of writing you in ink like a tattoo on my heart,
I'm afraid of every drip
            of my words because of the way
                    I melt under your eyes, I'm afraid of every
            you
that I write knowing that it's you I see stuck in time, but
            it's you I see in every phase of life,
                    it's you I see holding my hand
                            it's you at the end of the line,
                                    at the end of the day,
                                    at every end
                                            I don't know
                                            how to say.

So I let time wash over me and
worship its inconsistency and resist
the way my brain splits the present into three.
Afraid of the unknown but I'm trying to choose the now
and I'm painting it in the skies and sending
love notes to the ones who put me there.

I've forgone asking for permission to be happy
or expressing it in the right way.
I'm jumping
          barefoot
                    in puddles and
the ribbon
          in my hair
                    is only
                              getting
                                    longer.
There's kisses
                    on my
                              face from everyone
     I have the privilege
                                    to love
and I'm writing it all down
          and writing it all out
                    and writing it all for me.

Rescue Boat

I'll tell you something I mean,
just promise me you'll see it,

like a lighthouse
for this marsh we walk through.

And I won't rescue you
because you don't need me to

but if I find you on a lifeboat out at sea,
Would you tie it close to me?

Let me hold you close while
we each find our way back to be

and love me in the lighthouse
even when we haven't been lost at sea.

And I Fear Until I Dream

Scared that I'm not worth it
so I assume the worst, it
damages relationships faster than a fight.
My silent resignation snuffing out the light,

I extinguish the hope so I don't go up in flames.
I'm just afraid it will all be the same
but actuality and situations reveal the truth
where one was performance, what's true can all that undo.

Undoing the misconstrued narratives of what it takes to hold a
heart
as building myself back up from half has been a start,
but realizing you'll fight for me as my whole
and not just broken down to pieces to hold

inside when you need and want and I'm finally seeing.
Lately, I've been doing a lot of dreaming.

After it All

The doubt that choked Orpheus
will not have a hold on me.
He loved so hard only to find
himself drowned in it.

Let love become a person
and let me hold them in my arms.
I will not ask for answers
only that together we stay above ground.

I will not find myself drowned
by poetic musings of a love too large,
countered by a doubt too strong.
I will put down roots and entwine
myself with love and you;
settled, steady, sweet.

As branches stem from the tree
so do we extend to our own lives
and trust that we will come back
to roots in which we will settle in us.

I Settle in You

I think I'd rather light my tears on fire
and burn myself in the process
then admit that I'm scared.
My throat is filled with cement
    so I can only cough up
        half-finished sentences
  but if I rip
out all my hair and
        show you my brain (

        Would my declarations read like drivel?
        Would my madness be too much?
)

But once "I miss you" settled inside my skin
something in me cracked
        like a sinner in church
and I bled
    ink on the page saying
everything that I'd been afraid to say.

        Whispering secrets to the choir,
      I laid on this church floor and warmed
    the cold with my gushing heart. Antsy like
  the night before I'd get to see your face,
I don't crack
    like the walls of this church,
but I let it crumble
      all over
    me
    as if I did.

I settle in "I miss you" and I settle in you
and I'm waiting for the vines
that looped up   from   the garden
                in   my
                    heart
to let go
                        of my tongue so I can tell you
more words than a poem that's missing
                                    rhymes.

My words have been hidden (
                    in the
                    stubb-
                    ornly
                    still
                    lake
from fear of making
            waves and
                    not doing it
        right.
But I'll let the tears
        fall and
            float in
                    the river
                            they create.
            My strength in flames
    will give me a light in the dark
and when I find you
                    in the trees
I'll bend the
                    river like
        a willow and we'll
        find each other amidst the fears and tears and
years will go by but I'll always find us here.

So much saccharine lies in the thickness of the unknown
and I want to
                    wade through
        the marshes
                            with you
            as we discover
the joy in the constant change,
like the strands of your hair and the songs I like to play.

I Fall For You Like a Sailor to a Siren

I fall
             for you like a sailor to a siren
because even though I fall
             for you,
I fall
                              alone, knees
on the ground
                    and heart on the floor.
I try to mop
                    the blood up
             before you can see but you find
      a guilty look on my face
and my efforts are rendered futile.

I want to whisper the naked truths in your ear
             but like whispering into a seashell
                    the truth would echo
                              throughout the ocean.
             And so doubt
      creeps in and
screams louder than my voice.

Reality is pierced with visions of sailors
                                   drowned, I shove wax
             in my ears and I can't hear a sound.
      I'm afraid to love you out loud
so I close (my eyes as I fall
                    into doubt.
      But with my senses closed, still I could find you.

             I want to love you like Orpheus did Eurydice
      but I beg and plead the gods for a different end,

one where love exists   outside
        of mortals and myths and maybes.
)

Meet me in the forest and
        we'll seek counsel from the wood nymphs.
                This love came from the earth and
        to the earth it shall return.

It whispered to us from the trees we passed
        and will whisper to any other travelers
                finding this path by chance. Despite
        the weather-worn footprints
    they walk until feet become roots
and arms become branches.
        We will always come back here
                and here we will always be.

MY HEART WAS IN TUPPERWARE

MY HEART WAS IN TUPPERWARE—
Because I had slipped
    through the cracks
        in the table and caught it in (
                    cupped
        hands, it dripped
     down
       my
        arms   )
where it used to be
and I'm watching it seep into my skin under the sun.

YOU MADE ME FEEL LIKE I COULD TAKE OFF THE LID—
My skin is paper thin,
bones crack
    easier than a tree branch,
and my heart is glass.
But it's cracked
      before
       and I picked it up off the floor.
      I created it anew
    and am learning to honor its delicateness
and it feels safe with you.

Rough Draft

I'm always putting out fires till the flames
engulf me. I care too much and yet not
enough. I suffer under the cold stare of myself
when tired and resentful from helping someone else.

Because I'll break every wall down to get to them
but board up every door of my own, lest anyone
sees the way blood leaks out the cracks
or the way screams crack the walls.

I can't exist in fractures in my perfectly practiced
visuals. One crack and the whole thing falls,
one crack and I don't know where to go.
because then what was it all for?

Relentlessly pushing for others
to avoid my chaos and to make them believe
I'm the shoulder they can rely on.
I can't afford to crack but I can't afford to run.

The shadows I ignore follow me wherever I go
and it's only at night where I meet them,
and at night where I meet my end.

Tears in a Desert

We have plenty of time in the long term
to touch and feel and learn,
but my mind latches on short term
and I feel you slip away. I plant

hourglasses instead of flowers
counting the hours, falling
through my hands like sand,
I force the dirt between my toes to become

quicksand as I fail to stand with my hands
gripping my wrinkled heart
wishing you would wrench it away
and take back your clothes I bury myself in.

Pushing against this wall of trauma,
Do you see I'm trying? Am I
allowed to be in your arms crying?

when

you say you want me,
you say it with your eyes
and you touch your lips and i
feel you teasing mine.
you tell me you want me,
and i catch myself looking behind.

how could you love me so
gently and want me so
naturally at the same time?

i say i want you,
you can hear it in my tone,
and i touch my lips because i'm
 flustered all the time.
i tell you i want you and
your eyes stay locked on mine.

how could you love me so
strongly and loudly
when I'm used to loving alone?

i say i want you
you say you want me,
my body misses yours
but with you my heart is at home.

Painter's Palette of Ponderings

With speckled paint on your face
    and eyes a color I'll never be able to explain,
        you look like someone that would take years to
    create.
        A sketch that someone keeps
    coming back to,
a thought that will never be fully thought through.

You're easy to come back to and harder
                to leave,
but I'm afraid to tell you all this
because it feels so much like a test
    and with the wrong word or phrase
        I'll fail and all the paint
           will fall at my feet.

    What if you were never real?
    What if I don't deserve you here?
    It's getting harder and harder to have you
near but not

        here
among the cracks
        and blood
          of my heart,
but when I let you in,
    will you look at it and call it a mess?
        Or will you take off your shoes and dance in
    it too?

The Missing You Gets Louder

There's a rabbit hole of
  questions of *what if this?* and *what if that?*
    and *what if we could fall down?*
      but you hold a crystal in your hand
        and I write until my fingerprints are stained.

We're melting
    like cheese and kissing
        in swimming pools.
    and random things become more
  significant like the moments before ten pm when
I anticipate your call and to you, the water bottle
and Tums I left

    behind. I'm waiting for you
        to come around the corner and you're
    waiting for me to
  come back. Waiting and
    wanting and wishing

and swinging
     on the
        invisible string
you think I'm too blind to see.
But I see us leaving parts of our souls around
     the world, skipping stones and swinging
        on strings that will bend and
    mold but never break.

u & i

I wish I could protect you from the thorns of your own garden,
I wish I could rip them from the ground,

but it is not my place to run around.
So I hold you like you're my world and love you twice as hard,

I kiss your forehead when you speak of the trees towering
over you,
I hold your hand when the leftover flames

are creeping in. But we make a path in this forest,
For rest and love and life, and on this path I litter

rocks and pebbles and words and stories and lives
so that if one day you mistake them for a path to follow

and not a love to remember,
you'll still find me at the end.

I'll fill whatever plots of soil you give me
with the fresh seeds of my love.

I'll plant it over and over again as long
as you give me the chance.

And though to some this may be a secret place
it will be celebrated as loud as the lakes you run to

and stretch as far and as deep
for as long as you'll let me.

But already I feel you putting down roots,

laughing in the face of my requests,

I feel you holding me from behind, and I'm
holding your hand in mine until it's human

nature, until in whatever we can find
I'd feel your heart tugging the string of mine.

Just One

Let's say I want to write a poem about you.

I could write about your eyes, your hair, your neck,
 but none of that would come close to what I really mean.

I've written twenty messy poems trying to declare how I feel,
tapping into old codes of when my love would be tested
but you don't tie my hands behind my neck.

You don't force me into a confession booth and
twist my tongue until I manufacture half-truths and lies,
because how true could it be if it's not coming from me?
With you it lingers and festers and I can't coax it out,

I can figure it out because you've given me time,
I'm not forced to have words I just feel.
Like every great poet before me I muse.

Let's say I want to write a poem about you,

I'd write about how loving you feels like laughing.
I'd write about a thousand abstract things

because I can't nail it down.
This cliche of my floating heart bubbles whenever
you keep your wandering eyes on me.

I've fallen into these cliches and I curse myself for bad writing,
I cursed love poems and how naive they made me out to be
but you're the muse I keep coming back to write.
With freckles speckled like a curious painter,
you'd be the drawing they kept coming back to.

So let's say I want to write a poem about you, well,
I'd tell myself I'm crazy

I can't write just one.

Acknowledgements

I would like to take the time to extend my deepest gratitude to the following people who helped make this possible:

My beta readers– Maria Cangro, Paige Mathieu, Sonali Shah, Kristen Vincent, and Liz Moronski. You saw this at its barest and held it with the most gentle of hands. Thank you for seeing something in me and helping me be even better.

My first editor– Dakota Reed– It was a pleasure to connect with you through Reedsy. The care and investment you had for my work means more than you could know. Thank you for helping me to be bolder in my work.

My publisher– Angel Ackerman. You truly are an angel! Working with you has been one of the most exciting parts of my year. Your enthusiasm, excitement, and encouragement of me have been invaluable. I can't wait for all that's in store for us.

The whole team at Parisian Phoenix– Thank you for taking me in. Thank you for your respect and enthusiasm. I can't wait to keep working together.

The Lafayette English Club– The community and support I have found in everyone that I have met through this organization has meant more than even I realize. English lounge forever!

My teachers & mentors– Those of you that have sparked the passion of writing and reading in me hold one of the dearest places in my heart. Thank you for seeing me, for believing me and for taking me seriously as an artist. Your effect has been immeasurable and I hope to show you my gratitude in more ways than this.

My loved ones– Thank you for believing in me when I couldn't. It's no small feat sharing such vulnerable work as this, thank you to all those who let me read it to you in whatever state it fell on that day. I wouldn't want to create something like this if it wasn't to share and celebrate with you. Thank you for always seeing the best in me.

And to everyone else who has helped shape me as a person and an artist. Thank you. Thank you. Thank you.

MCKENNA GRAF is an undergraduate student studying English (Creative Writing Concentration) and Film & Media Studies at Lafayette College in Easton, Pa. She is incredibly involved in the arts community on campus and works tirelessly to support her fellow student artists.

She has attended the *Great Books Online Fiction Workshop* and *Kenyon Young Writers Workshop*. Her work has been featured in: *Creative Communications'* "A Celebration of Poets," *Live Poets Society of NJ's* "American High School Poets" Fall and Winter Anthology of 2020, *Bernards Township Library's* "Suzanne Cutler Teen Creative Writing Contest" of 2019 & 2020, and several editions of student run literary magazines.

In 2023 she self-published a poetry chapbook *writing over the word limit*. She is actively working to hone her craft and is spending all of 2024 submitting her work to literary journals for feedback as well as possible recognition. She has several short films in progress on her Vimeo and is interested in the intersection between film and poetry. You can follow along with her journey on Instagram @mckennagrafwrites or on her website www.mckennagraf.com

parisian phoenix
PUBLISHING

Similar titles from PPP:

TWISTS: Gathered Ephemera
darrell parry

REVISED AND EXPANDED SECOND EDITION NOW AVAILABLE

The Phulasso Devotional
Engineering the Warrior Priest for Dark Times
Thurston D. Gill Jr.

Not an Able-Bodied White Man with Money:
Expressions of Alternative Perspectives Influenced by Experiences in Lehigh Valley, Pennsylvania
EDITED BY Angel R. Ackerman

Purchase our titles on our website, online or ask for them at your favorite bookseller.

Subscribe to our Newsletter on
 substack

https://parisianphoenixpublishing.substack.com/